Career Quest

# EXPLORING SERVICE TRADES CAREERS

KELLEY BARTH

TWENTY-FIRST CENTURY BOOKS / MINNEAPOLIS

**To all of the frontline service professionals—thank you for making our world run smoother.**



Twenty-First Century Books™
An imprint of Lerner Publishing Group, Inc.
241 First Avenue North
Minneapolis, MN 55401 USA

For reading levels and more information, look up this title at www.lernerbooks.com.

Main body text set in Bembo Std Regular.
Typeface provided by Monotype Typography.

**Library of Congress Cataloging-in-Publication Data**

Names: Barth, Kelley author
Title: Exploring service trades careers / Kelley Barth.
Description: Minneapolis, MN : Twenty–First Century Books, [2026] | Series: Career quest | Includes bibliographical references and index. | Audience: Ages 11–18 | Audience: Grades 7–9 | Summary: "The service industry focuses on meeting peoples' needs. This vast field includes staff in hotels, restaurants, hair salons, and more. Learn all about these careers and how to join one"—Provided by publisher.
Identifiers: LCCN 2025011274 (print) | LCCN 2025011275 (ebook) | ISBN 9798765662694 library binding | ISBN 9798348029548 paperback | ISBN 9798765699942 epub
Subjects: LCSH: Service industries—Vocational guidance—Juvenile literature | Vocational guidance—Juvenile literature
Classification: LCC HD9981.5 .B375 2026 (print) | LCC HD9981.5 (ebook) | DDC 331.702—dc23/eng/20250417

LC record available at https://lccn.loc.gov/2025011274
LC ebook record available at https://lccn.loc.gov/2025011275

Manufactured in the United States of America
1 – CG – 12/15/25

# CONTENTS

# INTRODUCTION

"Good morning. What can I get for you today?" a friendly barista asks before taking down your morning coffee order. You watch as they froth the oat milk for your latte and call out your name with a smile.

You walk outside and run to the bus stop. Thankfully, you are just in time as the driver pulls up, opens the door, and gives you a wave to step inside. "Have a nice day," the bus driver says as you exit at the stop just down the block from your preferred hair salon.

As you sit down in the salon chair, enjoying the last sip of your latte, your hairstylist asks, "So, what are we doing today? The usual cut and color?" You relax, knowing you are in capable hands as they wash, trim, dye, and style your hair.

It is hard to get through a day without the help of people in the service industry. Just like the barista, bus driver, and hairdresser, service industry professionals provide help and assistance for customers and consumers in their daily lives. They are integral parts of making our world run smoothly

A barista prepares a morning coffee order for a waiting customer.

and successfully. Countless career options are available in the service industry. This book will help you learn more about these different careers and decide if a career in service might be right for you.

CHAPTER ONE

# At Your Service

Unlike manufacturing, the service industry consists of individuals and businesses providing services instead of products. But just as there are many kinds of products in the world, there are countless types of services that people seek out on a daily basis. The service industry is a massive source of jobs in the United States. In fact, a large and thriving service industry is one sign of a strong economy. More than one hundred million people work for private businesses that provide service. Chances are good that at some point in your life, you will have a job in the service industry. Maybe you already do!

The service industry encompasses many different types of work. Health care, education, public safety, media and entertainment, and finance are all common sectors within the service industry. Doctors, teachers, accountants, and firefighters all provide necessary services, not products. It would take many books, however, to cover all those various career pathways.

A makeup artist applies setting powder to complete their client's look.

Instead, this book will focus on some of the customer-facing service positions in popular fields such as hospitality and tourism and beauty and wellness. But don't forget, no matter what sector the job is in, if your goal is to help people, there is certainly a career in service that is right for you.

## Customer Service Skills

While the job duties may differ widely from one another, there are several personal traits and skills that will benefit you if you want a career in service. Providing quality customer service can make a huge difference for companies, customers, and in your own job satisfaction.

## Communication

Like in many careers, being a capable communicator is often the key to finding success in providing service. Service professionals need to understand their clients' needs and wants. They also need to be able to clearly communicate their services and policies in order to avoid problems or unmet expectations.

Hairstylists, for example, need to listen carefully and ask thoughtful questions to learn about what their clients want. The most fantastic style makeover in the world wouldn't be very appreciated if all the client wanted was a small trim. A waiter needs to be able to explain the menu options to an inquisitive diner. Even more importantly, they need to be able to clearly communicate with the kitchen staff about any food preferences or allergies.

Being confident in the way you communicate makes clients and customers feel confident as well. Successful service providers allow their customers to feel like they are understood and will be supported. Using active listening and speaking clearly and concisely will serve you well, even during busy, high-pressure situations.

## Attitude

One extremely important trait to bring to a career in service is a positive attitude. Not only will a positive outlook make you more appealing to customers, but it will also often make your time working more enjoyable. Being patient and empathetic and maintaining a positive attitude can help customers feel more comfortable and be more likely to return to your business in the future.

Think about the times when you most enjoyed interacting

**A team of baristas approach their work with friendly, positive attitudes. An interaction with a service professional can determine whether a customer will return to a coffee shop.**

with a service provider. What kind of attitude did they have? How did they speak to you? What kind of tone and body language did they use? How did they make you feel? If you're ever working with customers, try to model the qualities you appreciate.

## Resiliency

Customer service is often challenging. You have to deal with customers who are at their best and those who are at their worst. Simply put, sometimes you will run into an angry,

## Finding Creative Inspiration

Jobs in service are vital to making our world run, even if they aren't always thought of as high-powered or glamorous. Every job plays a role. And every role is a part of a bigger story. One famous story from the early 1960s demonstrates just how important and meaningful jobs in service trades can be.

President John F. Kennedy was visiting the National Aeronautics and Space Administration (NASA). The United States was deep into its twentieth-century Space Race rivalry with the Soviet Union (a former group of European countries including Russia) and desperately working to send astronauts to the moon. As the story goes, while touring the high-tech facility, the president came across a janitor carrying a broom. Kennedy curiously asked the man what he was doing. The janitor replied, "Well, Mr. President, I'm helping to put a man on the moon."

The janitor's response illustrates the important role service industry professionals play. Behind every massive accomplishment is a team of supporters taking care of all the small daily tasks that make companies and communities run smoothly.

rude, or difficult customer. Service jobs can also be physically and emotionally demanding. In many careers, you may have long hours working on your feet. You are expected to provide top-notch service even if you are tired or having a hard day. Determination, resilience, and a strong work ethic help keep successful service workers motivated even through

**Customer service can come with challenges, but trying to stay positive can help you overcome them.**

the challenging times. If you need to tap into your resilience, there are a few things you can try:

- Take a quick break.
- Confide in a trusted coworker.
- Think about all the reasons why you love your career.
- Focus on the successes, not the struggles.

### Resourcefulness

Customers want to feel confident that their service providers are competent and have the experience and knowledge to help them correctly. Service environments are often fast-paced, and customers will have different wants and needs. Being a flexible and strong problem-solver often comes in handy. Most service professionals will face new situations and challenges every day. Listening to clients and finding solutions to problems, even while busy or under stress, will help you succeed in a service-oriented career.

While strong customer service skills are necessary for anyone interested in a service industry career, don't fear if you aren't an expert yet! These skills develop over time. They take practice. Even after years of working in service, new situations will still find a way to challenge you and maybe even make you doubt your skills. Don't lean into that doubt, though. Facing new challenges is a useful way to keep building your service skills. If you are interested in further developing your skills, consider finding a mentor who has been in your desired career field for a few years. Learning alongside others is a helpful and motivating way to continue to grow throughout your career.

Wait staff often have to think and act quickly to manage multiple tasks at once.

CHAPTER TWO

# Careers in the Service Industry

The service industry includes countless career options. Each career has its own specific focus, demands, educational background, responsibilities, and work environment. Investigating different career options is a great way to start thinking about what path may be the best fit for your own interests and skills.

The hospitality and tourism industry, for example, thrives on providing quality and personalized customer service. This industry focuses on providing food, lodging, and entertainment to customers. Individuals working in the hospitality industry often serve as the hosts to their clients or guests to make sure they have a safe, enjoyable experience. Let's look at some specific jobs in hospitality and more.

## Lodging Service Careers

### Lodging Managers

Lodging managers oversee the daily running of hotels, motels, and resorts. They are in charge of managing staff, making sure

**Lodging managers often step in to help guests who run into a problem.**

that the facility is running smoothly, and helping respond to guest questions and concerns. Above all, lodging managers must make sure that their business is providing quality service by setting the tone for the entire establishment. Based on the needs of the particular business, lodging managers may have a variety of educational backgrounds. Some managers have a high school diploma and on-the-job training. Others have an associate's degree or certification in a related field. Most positions, however, would prefer to see a candidate with a bachelor's degree in hospitality or hotel management. Lodging managers typically make around $65,000 a year.

A hotel concierge can be a very helpful resource in discovering the local food and entertainment options.

## Front Desk Clerks

While a lodging manager is in charge of all the business's operations, a front desk clerk is often the first person you will see when you walk into a new hotel. Front desk clerks take reservations, check in guests, process payments, and handle basic requests. Most clerk positions require a high school diploma and on-the-job training. On average, front desk clerks make around $32,500 a year.

## Concierges

Many higher-end hotels and resorts also provide concierge services. A concierge serves as an expert in the local tourism options. They can provide restaurant recommendations, help arrange local transportation and tickets, and assist guests with most of their basic service needs. Most concierge roles do not require higher education. If you are the friend in your group who is always in the know and loves giving advice, a concierge role may be a good fit for you. They typically make around $40,200 a year.

### Housekeepers

Just like a janitor helped put a man on the moon, the hospitality industry couldn't exist without the hard work of housekeepers. Imagine what it would be like to visit a filthy hotel room that hadn't been cleaned after the previous few guests. That hotel would very likely soon gain a poor reputation and potentially even go out of business entirely. Housekeepers keep hotels clean and orderly. They clean and sanitize bathrooms, vacuum and dust hotel rooms, and take out the trash. Housekeepers also provide clean towels and make beds with freshly laundered bedding. On average, they make around $33,500 a year.

## Food Service Careers

### Food Preparation Services

If you like to work with your hands and are passionate about preparing meals for people, numerous jobs are available in the food industry. Most of these career options do not require formal education, although a degree from a culinary arts program is beneficial if you want to be in charge of a food preparation environment. Many chefs and head cooks do have such a degree. Head chefs are in charge of the kitchen and all food preparation. They plan menus, choose ingredients, monitor safety standards, and oversee and manage other staff.

The head chef is responsible for overseeing all food quality and presentation.

Chefs and head cooks make $59,000 a year on average.

Any well-run restaurant, kitchen, or cafeteria needs a strong support staff. Many levels of additional cooks report to the head chef or cook and assist in preparing meals. Cooks and other food preparation workers who aren't in a management role typically make around $32,420 a year.

On-the-job training is especially important in the field of food preparation. Often, even head chefs may start off their careers washing dishes or chopping vegetables. Driven and passionate workers are often able to move up into jobs with increased responsibilities and increased pay over time.

Do you prefer baking to cooking? There are plenty of positions open for passionate bakers as well. Like cooks, most positions do not require formal education, although many people who want to run or manage a bakery get a culinary degree. Bakers make an average of $35,000 a year.

## Servers

If you like the idea of being in the food service industry but aren't excited about making the food, hosting or serving may be right for you. Hosts greet customers, manage reservations, and seat guests. Servers, also commonly called waiters and waitresses, are the primary point of contact for diners. Servers are the important communication link between customers and the kitchen staff. They take orders, deliver food, and generally check in to make sure any customer needs are met. Servers do not need formal education and typically learn the necessary skills on the job. Servers often make minimum wages, which are supplemented through customer tips. On average, they make around $29,710 a year, although that

## Additional Careers in Care Service

Don't worry if a job in lodging or food services doesn't feel like the right fit for you. Many people are drawn to careers in care services based on their specific passions.

### Childcare Service

If you love working with young children, perhaps a career as a nanny, daycare provider, or working in an after-school program would be a good fit. Working with young children can be challenging, but it can also be very rewarding, and there is never a dull moment. Employees in this field must demonstrate an abundance of patience, energy, and creativity. Above all, childcare workers must place the highest importance on safety and security and have a deep love for children. Educational requirements vary by state and work environment. Many employers prefer to hire candidates with at least a high school diploma. However, a college degree or coursework, especially in the field of education, can be helpful if you are seeking a higher-level position. The average childcare worker makes about $30,000 a year.

### Animal Care Service

Like childcare, many people who love animals choose to pursue a career caring for them. Many people consider their pets an important member of their family, and they want to know that the people caring for them will be compassionate and diligent in their care. Jobs in pet training, grooming, walking, and boarding give employees the opportunity to provide a service for people while spending time with the animals they love. Caring for animals is a growing field, and the average employee makes approximately $32,000 a year.

### Plant Care Service

If you have a green thumb, there are also careers that allow you to serve others by working as a landscaper or groundskeeper. Landscapers plant and maintain trees, flowers, and other greenery. They are in charge of making sure that the landscaping around homes, apartments, and commercial buildings is beautiful and well-kept. Groundskeepers play a similar role focusing on upkeep of the outdoors. They also often help rake leaves, remove snow, and provide routine maintenance for outside structures such as playgrounds, benches, or fountains. Some groundskeepers specialize in maintaining locations such as cemeteries or athletic fields. Landscapers and groundskeepers do not need formal education, and they often gain their skills on the job. It helps to be prepared for hard physical labor and to enjoy working outdoors. On average, these plant care positions pay around $38,000 a year.

Someone who loves animals can choose from a variety of jobs involving pets of all species, shapes, and sizes.

number can vary depending on what type of restaurant they work in.

### Beverage Services

Other related food service career options include those in the beverage industry. Baristas, for example, take orders and make custom beverages for clients. Like most other servers, they often don't need formal education as on-the-job training is a great way to learn the ins and outs of beverage service. On average, beverage servers make $31,510 a year.

## Event Service Careers

The tourism and event industry also has several interesting career opportunities for people who want to share their specific passions with others.

### Event Planners

Event planners make sure that large events such as business conferences, conventions, and weddings run seamlessly. Event planners must be very detail-oriented as they oversee many event specifics such as venues, food, transportation, finances, and other logistics. Event planners must listen very closely to their clientele to ensure that they provide events services tailored to the client's individual needs. Event planners typically need a bachelor's degree and on-the-job experience. They make $57,000 a year on average.

### Travel Agents

If you are detail-oriented, good with research and budgeting, and love to travel, perhaps a career as a travel agent is the

Event planners must be very detail-oriented to ensure that an event's decorations are exactly what a client requested.

right path for you. While travel agents are sometimes able to visit specific destinations, they spend most of their time in an office environment advising others. Travel agents assist individuals, groups, and corporations in planning and booking travel arrangements. They can assist in booking flights, hotels, and entertainment options. Travel agents typically need a high school degree. Additional college coursework in the travel industry is often helpful in finding a job. Travel agents make about $47,000 a year.

### Tour Guides

If you are passionate about sharing unique experiences with a diverse group of people, perhaps a career as a tour guide is right for you. Tour guides often specialize in some element of the location where they work, whether that is local history, nature, or adventure activities. Tour guides do not typically need any higher education, although they should be experts in their given field. Tour guides make, on average, $40,300 a year.

## Careers in Beauty and Wellness Services

The beauty and wellness industry is another large source of service-driven careers. Individuals working in the beauty and wellness industry often need to keep up-to-date with style trends. They must also have impeccable service skills, as they work one-on-one with clients to provide very personal and often intimate services.

### Hairstylists and Barbers

Hairstylists and barbers provide direct services such as cuts, color, and styling to clients' hair. All hairstylists and barbers must be licensed in the state where they work. Specific licensing qualifications vary by state, but candidates in this field typically must have a high school diploma or a general education development (GED) certification, attend a state-licensed cosmetology or barber school, and pass an exam in order to begin working in the hair styling industry. On average, hairstylists and barbers make $35,000 a year, although their salary can vary based on the type of establishment they work at.

A barber carefully measures to make sure he gives his client an even hairstyle.

Nail technicians pay close attention to detail to make sure that they provide clients with the perfect style.

## Nail Technicians

Nail technicians provide manicure and pedicure services to clean, shape, and style fingernails and toenails. They also need to maintain the highest hygiene standards and follow health regulations. All nail technicians must be licensed in the state where they work. In order to be licensed, nail technicians must complete a cosmetology or nail technician program and pass a state exam. On average, nail technicians make around $34,000 a year.

## Massage Therapists

Massage therapists apply pressure and manipulate the body to help relieve pain, increase relaxation, and improve overall wellness for their clients. Most states require massage therapists to be licensed. Most massage therapists attend a postsecondary program where they complete traditional coursework and learn hands-on techniques. Massage therapists make $55,000 a year on average.

## Estheticians

Estheticians specialize in providing skin care services to clients. They often utilize facials, masks, peels, and scrubs to help improve the condition of a client's skin. Some estheticians also provide services for hair removal such as waxing or laser treatments. They also work with clients to determine their needs and what type of ongoing skin care would be best for them. Estheticians must attend a state-approved education program and pass an exam in order to become licensed to work. Estheticians typically make around $43,000 a year.

## Makeup Artists

Aspiring makeup artists have a number of different career opportunities to choose from. Some makeup artists specialize in consultations and makeup applications for clients. These artists spend much of their time helping individuals look their best for big events such as weddings. They also teach individuals what type of everyday makeup routines may work for their skin and preferences. Other makeup artists work in film, theatrical productions, or print media. These artists can do anything from applying basic makeup to a model about to walk the runway to adding an entire prosthetic face to transform an actor into an alien. Theatrical makeup artists work with creative teams to decide how they can use makeup to help tell a story. On average, makeup artists earn

Tattoo artists need to be well-versed in safety and health precautions, such as proper hygiene and protective equipment.

around $68,600 a year. Makeup artists who work in the entertainment industry typically earn more than those who work with individual clients.

### Tattoo Artists

Like other professionals in this field, tattoo artists use their creative eye to help deliver a style that their clients are looking for—only a tattoo artist's designs are permanent. Some states require aspiring tattoo artists to undergo an apprenticeship that can take several months. All states, however, require tattoo artists to be licensed and trained in certain safety procedures. The average tattoo artist makes around $64,000 a year.

No matter if you are interested in hospitality, beauty and wellness, or care, the service industry could use your specialized interests and skills. The next chapter will go into further detail to help you find what service industry role might best suit you.

CHAPTER THREE

# How May I Help You?

If you are interested in a career in the service industry but aren't certain about what pathway is right for you, think about the specifics of each career. How many years of education do you want to pursue after high school? What kind of work environment and schedule do you want? Do you want to work with a specific population such as children or animals? Do you like having a wide variety of tasks in your day-to-day schedule, or do you prefer to specialize in one area or skill? Do you see yourself as an artist? Do you prefer to be in nature? Whatever your interests and preferences, there is probably a service industry career out there that is right for you.

## Career Assessments

Understanding your passion is a great way to start narrowing down your career choices. Try making a list of your favorite activities and hobbies. What do you enjoy about these activities? What do they have in common? Are you the friend

Taking time to analyze your skills and interests can assist you in choosing the right career path.

in the group with a well-established skin care routine who is always offering advice to others? Or are you more of a planner who loves a themed party and can create a stunning balloon arch? Perhaps a career as an esthetician or event planner is the right way for you to put your passions to work. Don't be afraid to think outside the box!

It might be worth your time to take some self-assessments to learn more about how your skills and interests may translate into different career pathways. Don't worry, these aren't tests that you need to study for. In fact, they can be an interesting way to discover yourself and your priorities on a

Hotel housekeepers must work quickly to prepare rooms so the next guests can check in.

deeper level. The CareerOneStop website offers an interest assessment and a skills assessment. These both offer a quick quiz that will give you results about what career areas might suit you. You can also create a free account at the MyACT website. This site has a variety of personal inventories that will help you map out and understand how your skills, interests, and values relate to different career opportunities.

## Work Environments and Schedules

When choosing a career, it is important to look at the work environment and schedule and think about how that career could fit in with your desired lifestyle. Some people like a lot of variety, while others prefer to do the same thing each day. Some people prefer to have a standard work schedule. Others enjoy the flexibility in choosing their own hours. Many people enjoy a fast-paced, busy work environment where there is always something to do. Others find that stressful and prefer to take their time in a slower environment. There is quite a bit of variety in the schedules of service workers. What type of schedule and environment do you prefer?

Depending on a person's specific job, there is typically a lot of variety in the day-to-day work in the service industry. Working with different people often helps make every day unique. The work environments and schedules of service workers can also vary widely. Service employees work in restaurants, hotels, salons, and other retail environments. These positions are good for people who like to have one location that serves as a home base. While the customers and clients will come and go, employees in these service careers will consistently work at the same location.

## Tip-Based Income

Wealthy American tourists first observed tipping in Europe and brought the practice to the US in the 1850s.

Most people you ask probably have strong opinions on tipping. *Tipping is out of control. If you can't afford to tip, you shouldn't go out to eat. Tipping should be mandatory. Tipping should be illegal.* You are likely to hear a lot of opinions about tipping culture and even more confusion. *Who exactly do you tip? How much should you tip? Do you have to tip even if you had bad service?* It is a complex topic that even has politicians debating about the future of tipping in the United States.

A tip is an extra financial amount that a customer decides to add for the service they were provided. But while it may be controversial, many service industry jobs heavily rely on the money that comes from tips. In some states, there is a guaranteed minimum wage, and any tips an employee may earn are on top of their base salary. That can mean good money for a lot of service workers. However, not all states have that minimum salary protection. Many waiters in particular work for less than minimum wage and rely on tips to supplement their base income. While the law requires servers to still make minimum wage, inconsistent tips can make it challenging for workers to pay their bills and budget.

Regardless of how you feel about tipping, the fact is that the amount of tips a worker receives can vary widely from day to day. It is best to plan for this fluctuation when you are choosing a tip-based career and budgeting for your lifestyle.

**A cruise ship worker helps load passenger luggage before a long voyage.**

But there are also plenty of opportunities for travel or outdoor work in certain service professions. In fact, many service careers are defined by how they support travel. Flight attendants, bus and taxi drivers, and cruise ship directors all specialize in serving travelers on the go. If you are looking for a career where you get to interact with people while always being on the move, a traveling service career like this might be just the ticket.

Much of the service industry doesn't take a day off. Thinking about your preferred work schedule is an important part of choosing a service career and job position that is best

## Self-Employment in the Service Industry

Being self-employed has a number of pros and cons. Self-employed service workers, such as a tattoo artist or tour guide who runs their own business, get to choose their own hours and work schedules. They have complete control over what projects they choose to take on and who they choose to work with. This can create a sense of pride and freedom for many people. Self-employment is particularly common in the beauty and wellness industry, where almost 50 percent of hairstylists and 80 percent of barbers are self-employed.

However, being self-employed also comes with challenges. When you are self-employed, you are in charge of every aspect of your company. Whereas larger companies have whole teams to market their services, manage budgets, and help provide service, self-employed individuals have to take on all those tasks themselves. Self-employment can also be challenging from a logistical perspective. You do not always get a steady paycheck, and you won't receive other benefits such as employer-sponsored insurance or paid time off. It can be a high-risk but high-reward situation.

for you. Many restaurant, lodging, and retail employees work in shifts—for example, throughout the daytime, evening, and even overnight. Many service jobs require working evenings, weekends, and sometimes even holidays. Consider what scheduling needs you have and how a particular career might support them. Finding how to balance your work life with your personal life is an important skill for most service workers.

Many disc jockeys, or DJs, are self-employed and get to choose when and where they work.

Strong customer service skills can help de-escalate a difficult situation.

## Work Challenges

Service industry workers face a variety of physical and emotional challenges in their line of work. Many service professionals have physically active jobs that require a lot of standing, walking, bending, and moving. It is important to take care of yourself, even as you take care of the customers and clients you are providing a service for. Service professionals should make sure that they find ways to minimize the strain that work puts on their bodies. For some professions that require a lot of standing, that could mean using an anti-fatigue mat and solid, supportive shoes to help with leg strain. In all professions, taking breaks to rest and recharge is important for your physical and mental health.

Another work challenge that often arises for people working in the service industry is facing upset or dissatisfied customers. An employee getting upset or angry will often only escalate a tense or challenging situation. Instead, try to practice patience, understanding, and empathy when dealing with difficult customers and situations. Successfully handling customer complaints goes a long way, not only toward satisfying customers in the moment, but also making them loyal customers who are more likely to return to your business. For example, the *Harvard Business Review* studied how companies responded to customer tweets. They found that "a mere acknowledgement of the customer's problem can defuse initial frustration and put the customer back on the road to loyalty. Instead of the customer seeing the company as the enemy, a sympathetic response can reorient the situation so that the customer now feels that the company is on his or her side."

CHAPTER FOUR

# Jump-Starting Your Career

You've decided that you are interested in a career in the service industry, but how do you go about actually starting one of these jobs? You don't have to wait to pursue your service career pathway. Between classwork, extracurricular activities, and part-time jobs, there are plenty of ways to start pursuing your passion.

## High School Coursework

Specific careers in the service industry each have different educational requirements. A few jobs are available even without a high school diploma. However, in almost all fields, completing high school or a GED is a good place to start. Having a diploma will often open up more opportunities for you and help you land that coveted job. Future service providers can learn a lot from all sorts of different class subjects.

### Art

A strong artistic eye can be especially helpful for certain

If you love art, there are a number of service careers that may be a good fit for your interest.

careers in the beauty industry such as makeup and tattoo artists or nail technicians. Honing your skills in drawing and color theory can be very useful when designing the right looks for clients and translating their preferences and visions.

## Business

At their heart, most service careers are grounded in business principles. Courses such as entrepreneurship or business leadership will help prepare you for a career and develop your customer service skills. This is especially important if you think you may want to be self-employed and run your own business someday. Courses in personal finance and budgeting will also help you develop the business savvy and money management skills you will need in your career.

## English, Speech, and Communications

Service providers must be clear communicators. Individuals need to be able to clearly articulate a business's rules and services. They also need to be able to empathize and understand a customer's needs so they can provide the right service. Developing your public speaking and writing skills

Developing your problem-solving skills will come in handy in many service careers.

will help set you apart and prepare you to deliver the highest quality customer service.

## Family and Consumer Science

Depending on your desired service career, family and consumer science classes can provide solid introductions to some of the specialized knowledge and skills you may need for the future. Coursework in the culinary arts or in childcare and development are particularly helpful if you are looking to go into those lines of work.

## Math

Basic math will come in handy in nearly all service careers. Many service providers handle payments and money from customers. Managing money well goes a long way in helping to assure customers that you and your business are trustworthy. Creating and overseeing budgets will also be beneficial if you are ever interested in moving into a managerial position. Beyond money management, mathematical skills are helpful whether you are baking a wedding cake, mixing up the right formula of hair dye, or measuring a backyard garden to determine how many bushes you will need to plant to fill the space.

## Technology

As service careers look toward the future, advancing technology will continue to impact many of the roles and duties of employees. Basic typing and computer skills will likely benefit you regardless of your chosen career path. Some passionate technology users even turn their interests into a full-time service career providing computer, phone, and tech support to customers.

A summer job at a youth camp is a great way to start your service career.

## World Languages

As our world is becoming more interconnected and linguistically diverse, being able to speak more than one language could be a substantial benefit working in the service industry. People of all linguistic backgrounds seek out services, and if you are able to connect in a customer's native language, it will help you become a more versatile, highly desired employee. Approximately one in five people in the United States speak a language other than English at home. Spanish is the second most popular language spoken by far. But Mandarin, Tagalog, Vietnamese, and Arabic are also common. Consider studying an additional language—or more—if you want to help provide services to a wider audience.

## Extracurricular Opportunities

Coursework is an important place to start as you prepare for a career in the service industry. However, there are also plenty of opportunities to get involved and learn more outside a traditional classroom. After all, many of the skills you need in a service industry career are learned through on-the-job experience. Take some time to evaluate all the skills and experience you already have and start brainstorming ideas to gain more.

### First Jobs

Many people's very first jobs are in the service industry. Part-time job opportunities are often available to high school students and can be a great way to hone your customer service skills and build your résumé. Working as a cashier, as a junior camp counselor, in a retail store, or in a fast-food restaurant are all practical ways to start your service career. Getting experience working with and serving the public will help you develop the communication, positive attitude, resiliency, and resourcefulness needed to succeed in the workforce. Having this early experience may also help you decide what type of service career would suit you best.

### Chores and Hobbies

Even many chores around the house are good for building your service skills. Babysitting the neighbor kids can help you build your résumé of skills to work as a nanny or in a childcare setting. Mowing the lawn and pulling weeds teaches you some of the

## Should You Go to College?

You may be questioning whether it is worth it to attend college if you are interested in a service career. College takes time and money. It is a good idea to think about your particular career goals when deciding if a two-year or four-year degree would be worthwhile and beneficial to your future.

Some jobs require you to have some additional schooling after high school but not a college degree. Instead, these programs are often focused on developing specific hands-on skills, last one year or less, and help prepare you for a licensing exam so you can become a hairstylist, massage therapist, nail technician, or esthetician, for example. Beyond these specific requirements, many service positions do not require any higher education. However, there are benefits to still earning a college degree.

In many careers, having a college degree is helpful when you are just starting off. Degrees in hospitality administration, event planning, tourism and travel management, business administration, and culinary arts can help you develop the right skill sets to get hired. College coursework can be especially important if you want to work at a higher-end establishment. A college degree can also be beneficial later in your career. A formal degree often makes it more likely that you would be eligible for future promotions or managerial roles. If you want to be a head chef or run a hotel, a college degree will often be necessary. Regardless of what educational pathway you choose, there is still nothing quite like on-the-job experience for growing your customer service skills.

Something you enjoy doing, such as lawn maintenance, could evolve into a future career in the service industry.

ins and outs of landscaping. Even doing the dishes or making your bed can prepare you for working in a kitchen or doing housekeeping. Think about all the chores and tasks you typically do in a week if you are worried about finding that first job without any previous experience. If you sit down to think about it, you may find that you have more experience and more skills than you realize.

Hobbies can also be inspirational jumping off points when preparing for your career path. Do you like cooking? Baking? Experimenting with new hair or nail styles? You never know—maybe you can turn your love of scrolling Airbnb listings into a thriving travel agent career!

CHAPTER FIVE

# The Future of Service with a Smile

The service industry is growing. The Occupational Outlook Handbook (OOH) maintained by the US Bureau of Labor Statistics predicts that the majority of service industry careers discussed in this book are expected to grow faster than average between 2023 and 2033.

A few particular careers have especially high demand and huge growth opportunities. Massage therapist roles and careers in animal care, for example, are predicted to grow by 18 and 15 percent respectively during this same period. Nail technicians, estheticians, lodging managers, and head chef roles are also expected to vastly outpace the average career growth in upcoming years.

Some service positions are not actively growing as fast as normal, however. The OOH says of restaurant serving careers, for example, that "reduced need for these workers is expected due to increases in the use of self-service technology, such as kiosks that allow customers to order and pay for food, and in carryout." The number of childcare positions are also shrinking because of a slowing birth rate,

As people prioritize self-care, there is an increasing demand for massage therapists and similar, relaxation-focused careers.

which means there are fewer young children who need care. But regardless of what specific service career you are interested in, chances are good that there will continue to be at least demand and even growth in most fields.

## Changing Technology in the Service Industry

In addition to growing quickly, the service industry is also always changing. This is part of what makes these jobs so appealing. An important part of a service worker's job is to stay up-to-date on the technology, trends, and changes in the field.

If you have ever scanned a QR code to see a restaurant's menu or checked into a hotel room with just your phone as a key, you are already seeing the effects of how technology is impacting the service industry. Author Nick Greenhalgh further explained how changing technologies such as artificial intelligence (AI) may impact the hospitality industry in an article for the University of Denver's Daniels College of Business: "This might look like an automated hotel check-in kiosk or AI-powered chatbots to communicate with guests. In the restaurant industry, it could appear as food preparation robots or an AI ordering agent to streamline operations for the drive-through window."

Technology is also impacting the beauty and wellness industry. Social media has been a hugely successful vehicle for beauty and wellness service providers to market their services. Technology advancements are also leading the industry to provide more personalized products and services for clients. As the author Advone Katsande put it, "From digital skin analysis to shade-matching foundation—the emergence of beauty tech has led to a more personalised shopping experience."

While this changing technology has the potential to make serving customers less expensive and more efficient, there are also potential concerns about the impact of AI. Some people are worried that AI will take over human jobs. Other experts disagree. They caution that jobs aren't going to be lost to AI, but instead will change and evolve.

AI is a powerful tool. But at the end of the day, it is just a tool that needs a person to run it. Humans bring an important

QR codes have helped change the way many service businesses run. What new technology might change things next?

## The Gig Economy

One increasingly popular career option for many people is finding jobs in the gig economy. As described on the job search website Indeed, "Gig jobs are on-demand roles that individuals can take as freelancers or independent contractors." Gig workers are not formally employed by a company either full-time or part-time. Instead, they set their own hours and work schedules and decide what work they want to take on. This high level of flexibility can be very appealing, and it is common for people to work one or even multiple gig opportunities in addition to their main career. Common gig roles include working as a rideshare driver, food delivery driver, or grocery service shopper. Working in a gig economy role can have similar benefits and challenges to being self-employed. There is a lot of freedom and flexibility, but you won't qualify for benefits such as health insurance or paid time off. Regardless, these jobs can be a great way to build up your customer service experience, especially if you are looking for something flexible and part-time.

Recording a voice-over for a television ad is an example of a gig job.

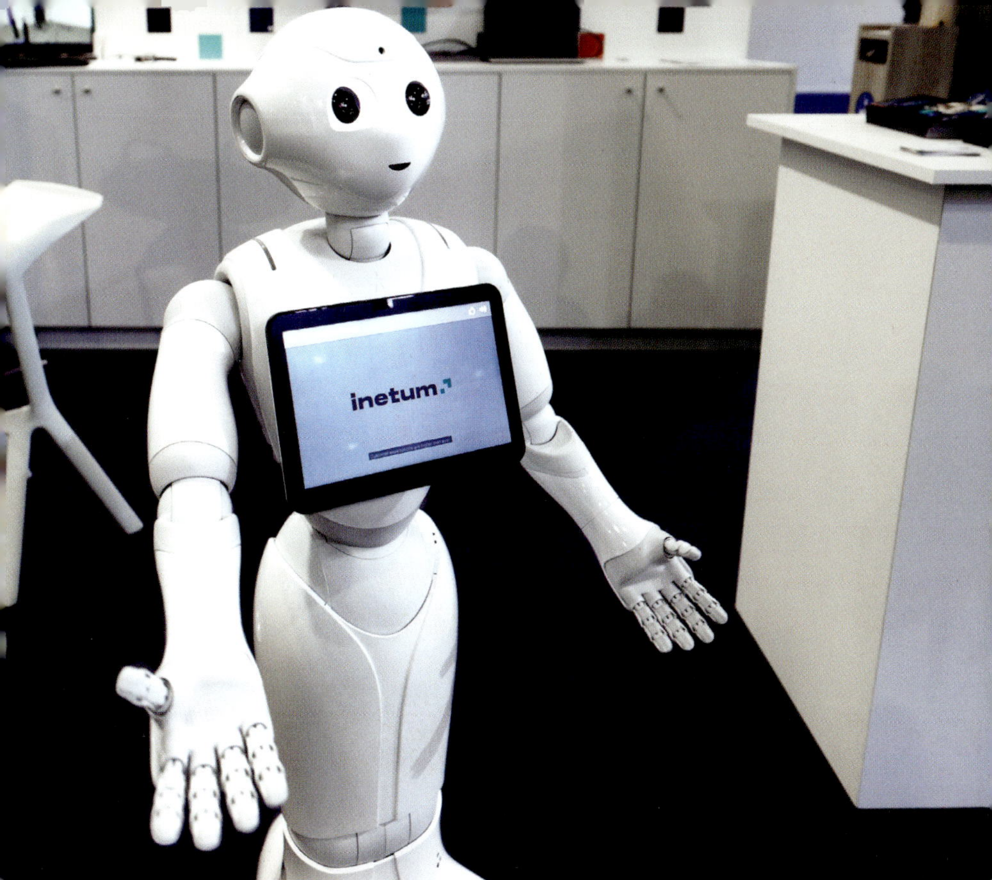


**Future service professionals will need to know how to efficiently work with AI technologies.**

understanding and personalized touch to the business of service that AI isn't likely to replicate. Boston University's School of Hospitality Administration agrees, saying that despite the fact that "robot greeters, housekeeping robots, and cooking robots have become more and more common in restaurants and hotels," AI isn't going to fully replace human jobs. "Instead, robots help us create a happier work environment with higher efficiency and enable us to allocate more time to connect with customers." So, embracing technology and staying up-to-date on how to best incorporate it into your workplace will likely be an important job skill for the future.

CONCLUSION

# Following Your Passion

Whether it's an after-school job or a full-time career, there are many jobs in the service industry available for people who enjoy working with others. While a career in the service industry can be challenging, with long hours and demanding work, it is also very rewarding for many people. Service workers can truly impact people's lives.

The best service providers know that they are never done learning and growing in their field. Practice and experimentation are crucial to improving your technical and customer service skills. Embrace the idea of always trying something new, especially the things that scare you. Try cooking with a new ingredient that may seem intimidating. Practice a new nail design that you've never mastered. Be open to learning from those around you—everyone has something new to learn, just as everyone has an insight or skill to teach.

In order to succeed in a demanding field, it's important to be passionate about your line of work. Think about the reasons that are drawing you toward a career in the service

**All jobs have challenges. What motivates you to push through the challenges and provide excellent service?**

industry. Try making a list of what is most important to you in your service career. Having a set of core values supporting your career path will help you to stay motivated and excited even on your challenging days. All jobs have their ups and downs, but having passion for what you do helps make it all worth it.

# GLOSSARY

**clientele:** a group of clients or customers

**compassionate:** offering sympathy for others' suffering and a desire to help

**coveted:** something that is deeply wished for or sought after

**culinary:** relating to cooking

**customer service:** providing assistance or help to the people who visit a business

**determination:** the act of making a firm decision

**diligent:** making a steady and earnest effort

**economy:** the structure or conditions of the financial system

**efficiency:** the quality of producing positive results without wasting time or energy

**empathize:** to be sensitive to and understanding of another's feelings or experience

**entrepreneurship:** the activity of creating your own business

**freelancers:** independent workers who are not affiliated with any specific business or organization

**gig economy:** jobs that offer short-term contracts or freelance work

**hospitality:** the business industry that provides services to guests typically in hotels and restaurants

**linguistic:** relating to spoken language

**lodging:** temporary sleeping accommodations

**managerial:** relating to the process of overseeing and running a business

**manufacturing:** the process of making and producing batches of apparel items

**passionate:** filled with an intense feeling or belief

**patience:** the trait of being able to wait or endure challenge without complaint

**resiliency:** the ability to recover or adjust to change

**sector:** an area or subdivision of a business industry

**tips:** extra money given to an employee by a customer for providing a service

**tourism:** relating to the field of travel

# SOURCE NOTES


39 "a mere acknowledgement . . . or her side": Wayne Huang, John Mitchell, Carmel Dibner, Andrea Ruttenberg, and Audrey Trippl, "How Customer Service Can Turn Angry Customers into Loyal Ones," *Harvard Business Review*, January 16, 2018, https://hbr.org/2018/01/how-customer-service-can-turn-angry-customers-into-loyal-ones.

50 "This might look . . . the drive-through window.": Nick Greenhalgh, "6 Trends in the Hospitality Industry," *Daniels College of Business*, August 8, 2024, https://daniels.du.edu/blog/trends-in-hospitality-industry/.

50 "From digital skin . . . personalised shopping experience.": Advone Katsande, "Beauty Tech: The Rise of Technology in the Beauty Industry," *Beauhurst*, March 16, 2023, https://www.beauhurst.com/blog/rise-of-beauty-tech/.

52 "Gig jobs are . . . or independent contractors.": Indeed Editorial Team, "35 Gigs Jobs To Explore (With Benefits and Tips)," Indeed, August 18, 2024, https://www.indeed.com/career-advice/finding-a-job/gig-jobs.

53 "robot greeters, housekeeping . . . connect with customers.": "Technology Shaping the Future of the Hospitality Industry," Boston University School of Hospitality Administration, January 26, 2023, https://www.bu.edu/hospitality/2023/01/26/technology-trends-in-hospitality/.

# SELECTED BIBLIOGRAPHY

"Food Preparation and Serving Occupations." Occupational Outlook Handbook. Updated August 29, 2024. https://www.bls.gov/ooh/food-preparation-and-serving/home.htm.

Huang, Wayne, John Mitchell, Carmel Dibner, Andrea Ruttenberg, and Audrey Tripp. "How Customer Service Can Turn Angry Customers into Loyal Ones." Harvard Business Review, January 16, 2018. https://hbr.org/2018/01/how-customer-service-can-turn-angry-customers-into-loyal-ones.

Indeed Editorial Team. "35 Gig Jobs to Explore (With Benefits and Tips)." Indeed. Updated August 18, 2024. https://www.indeed.com/career-advice/finding-a-job/gig-jobs.

"Personal Care and Service Occupations." Occupational Outlook Handbook. Updated August 29, 2024. https://www.bls.gov/ooh/personal-care-and-service/home.htm.

# FURTHER INFORMATION

## Books

Barth, Kelley. *Exploring Health-Care Careers*. Minneapolis: Twenty-First Century Books, 2026.
Medical professionals provide another kind of service: health care. This book explores a variety of health-care jobs.

Klatte, Kathleen A. *Cosmetologist*. Buffalo: Rosen, 2025.
This resource offers in-depth information about pursuing a beauty and wellness service career in cosmetology.

Muchnick, Justin Ross. *Teens' Guide to College and Career Planning: Your High School Roadmap to College and Career Success*. Denver: Peterson's, 2022.
This book is a guide to planning for college and learning how it will help you meet your career goals.

Sheen, Barbara. *What Now?: A Teen Guide to Life after High School*. San Diego: ReferencePoint Press, 2024.
Full of helpful advice, this book guides readers through making life and career decisions after high school.

Williams, Morgan. *Careers for People Who Love Cooking*. New York: Rosen, 2021.
This title details a variety of career opportunities available in the food service industry.

Williams, Morgan. *Careers for People Who Love Traveling*. New York: Rosen, 2021.
This book focuses on careers that provide an opportunity for travel.

## Websites

Careers and Career Information

https://www.careeronestop.org

CareerOneStop hosts this resource, providing self-assessment quizzes and a large variety of career information.

Hospitality Industry: Restaurants, Hotels, & Lodging Resource Guide

https://guides.loc.gov/hospitality-restaurants-hotels/introduction

The Library of Congress has a comprehensive collection of links and resources to learn more about the hospitality industry.

MyACT

https://my.act.org

This resource offers self-assessment quizzes and provides advice about how they relate to career and college opportunities.

Research Guides: Beauty

https://libguides.usc.edu/industries/beauty

This site from the University of Southern California Libraries provides an overview of online resources that are helpful in researching and keeping up with the beauty and wellness service industry.

Restaurant Industry Job Descriptions

https://restaurant.org/education-and-resources/learning-center/workforce-engagement/restaurant-industry-job-descriptions/

The National Restaurant Association offers detailed descriptions of different restaurant industry career options.

# INDEX

# ABOUT THE AUTHOR

Kelley Barth is a former children's librarian who loves connecting with young people over stories and books. When she isn't busy writing, she enjoys reading, hiking, crafting, and going on adventures with her husband and son.

# PHOTO ACKNOWLEDGMENTS

Image credits: Tom Werner/Getty Images, p. 5; Westend61/Getty Images, p. 7; Me 3645 Studio/Getty Images, p. 9; Klaus Vedfelt/Getty Images, p. 11; andresr/Getty Images, p. 13; Anchiy/Getty Images, p. 15; Thomas Barwick/Getty Images, p. 16; Nick White/Getty Images, p. 18; Jacob Wackerhausen/Getty Images, p. 21; Kosamtu/Getty Images, p. 23; Giselleflissak/Getty Images, p. 25; happy_finch/Getty Images, p. 26; Natalia Lebedinskaia/Getty Images, p. 28; fotostorm/Getty Images, p. 31; Hispanolistic/Getty Images, p. 32; monkeybusinessimages/Getty Images, p. 34; Holger Leue/Getty Images, p. 35; Smile/Getty Images, p. 37; richyrichimages/Getty Images, p. 38; Maskot/Getty Images, p. 41; monkeybusinessimages/Getty Images, p. 42; kali9/Getty Images, p. 44; fozzyb/Getty Images, p. 47; Thomas Barwick/Getty Images, p. 49; LeoPatrizi/Getty Images, p. 51; Hill Street Studios/Getty Images, p. 52; NurPhoto/Contributor/Getty Images, p. 53; ER Productions Limited/Getty Images, p. 55.

Cover image: Drazen Zigic/Getty Images